Time Management:

The Time Famine Solution

Laurie Leiker and Suzie Kummins-Poirier

DEDICATION

To all the time-starved, time-deprived, rushed, harried and hassled.

CONTENTS

ACKNOWLEDGMENTS

We'd like to acknowledge the help of all those we've relied on as we've put together this book. There are so many who have been a part of the process of putting together the information included in the book as well as those who support us in our day-to-day lives. We thank our families and significant others, our children and our parents. We thank all the bosses we've had in the past who have been nightmares when it comes to time management and all those we've been able to help through the years.

We'd also like to thank our online family, including Lori Shemek, Bob Choat, Amanda Quraishi, Tom Myer and Susan Irby. We may never have actually met you in person, but you're as much family to us as if we were born and raised in the same home. You mean so much to us and we could never do this without you.

1 WHY MANAGE YOUR TIME?

Time management. We each get 24 hours in a day, so why do we feel we don't have enough. It's like money; you can never have enough money or enough time, right?

Yet with time, as with money, we have the means of being able to use it wisely. That's not to say that every minute needs to be spent in a productive, concrete way; it means we need to make sure that were using the majority of our time wisely.

Time is our most important asset, even more important than money. You can always earn more money or spend less money, but you still only have 24 hours in a day.

Think about the times when you have been most productive. You were refreshed, focused and completely on task, with little or no interruptions.

To be successful, you need to use your time wisely. But does it follow that those who are successful use their time wisely? Not always. As matter of fact, some people are successful despite not knowing the first thing about using your time wisely. Imagine how much better and more successful they would be if they also use that time wisely.

TIME MANAGEMENT BENEFITS YOU:

- ✓ More control of your time and your life
- ✓ Increased recognition and reward with higher personal productivity levels
- ✓ Improved relationships both on and off the job
- ✓ Reduced stress and more enjoyment of everyday life

"I'm definitely going to take a course in time management...just as soon as I can work it into my schedule." Louis Borne

2 THE TIME FAMINE

Most of us are in a time famine. What does that mean? As we said, we feel as if we never have enough time to get done everything that needs to be done in a day. But  does that mean that you're running out of time? Let's take a look:

- Most US workers waste two hours every workday. Not every moment must be productive, but think about what you could accomplish with those 10 extra hours every week. Your deadlines would be met, meetings would be more productive, innovation would increase and you would feel less stressed.

- Sure signs of a time famine include:
  - ✓ Disorganized or unorganized inbox.
  - ✓ Cluttered desk.
  - ✓ Missed meetings or are unprepared for meetings.
  - ✓ Volunteering to do things other people could/should do.
  - ✓ Tired, unable to concentrate and STRESSED.

Wouldn't it be wonderful to not have to go through all the stress of the time famine?

Meeting your commitments or not speaks volumes about your intentions. If you are consistently missing time limits or deadlines, delaying outcomes or otherwise procrastinating, what message are you giving?

We are constantly inundated with requests for our time and expertise but when you overcommit or plainly don't back up your word with actions, you are shortchanging everyone - yourself, your clients, partners or colleagues. Consider message you're sending when you don't deliver the promised results at the promised time.

"Deadlines aren't bad. They help you organize your time. They help you set priorities. They make you get going when you might not feel like it. And meeting deadlines successfully is one of the best motivating factors out there." Harvey Mckay

3 THE BIGGEST KEY: PAY ATTENTION

Like money, time can fly away when you're not paying attention. So think about how much better things would be if you merely paid attention to what you were doing every day. I'm not talking keeping track of each second forever; but what would happen, how much time would you recoup if you paid attention for a week? You might say it would take too much time that you don't already have, but does it really?

According to research by Harmon.ie, workplace distractions cost U.S. businesses \$10,375 per employee each year.

"We can lay much of the blame on digital alerts and disturbances. Twenty-one percent of productivity losses are due to information overload -- that includes the onslaught of email, instant messages, cellphone alerts or phone calls, social media updates and RSS feeds."[1]

---

[1] http://blogs.payscale.com/salary_report_kris_cowan/2012/05/workplace-distractions-infographic.html

Here are some simple ways of figuring out where your time is going:

<u>Take control of your day, don't let your day control you</u>. You get into work and suddenly, your deadlines are in front of you, people are coming into your office and emails are flying all around you. Your day is already out of control. But it's only out of control because you haven't grabbed the reigns.

- ✓ Are you able to turn off or lower the volume of the notifications?
- ✓ Can you schedule 3-4 times throughout the day to review/respond to emails?
- ✓ Do you need to respond immediately to each byte of data that crosses your desk or your Smartphone?

Remember: YOU have the power to control your day. Just do it.

<u>Daily set priorities and manage your time to meet deadlines</u>. By taking time every day to set YOUR priorities, you feel less stressed; you know what needs to be done, you are getting your tasks done on your time, and everyone else's priorities will fill in around it.

Think of it this way: Imagine an empty mayonnaise jar, 6 ping pong balls and enough sand to fill the jar. If you fill the jar with the sand first, you might get one or two ping pong balls in there, but not all 6. But look what happens when you put the ping pong balls in first – pouring the sand in, you find not only do you have all your ping pong balls safely within the jar, but all the sand fills in around it.

The ping pong balls are your priorities for the day; if you have those set up and you're focusing on those items, everything else, the sand that is everyone else's priorities, will fill in around it. It's just that easy.

- ✓ Know which projects require the most time and your undivided attention.
- ✓ Create your boundaries for working hours and "publicize" them.
- ✓ Tune out distractions.
- ✓ Stay on task.

Goals

Effectively plan each hour, each day, each week by setting and achieving goals. So many times, we find ourselves going through life without any real goals. "But wait," you might say. "I know I want to be successful and rich without any stress in my life; that's a goal." True, but it's too nebulous; there's nothing concrete to achieve.

Goals need to be achievable. Goals can be large (I will get a well-deserved raise by the end of the year) or small (Today, I am going to thank one team member for their hard work), but they're achievable, reasonable and likely to occur if you focus on them.

Goals need to be written down every day. Each day should have its own goal, even if it's to have your desk cleared off before you leave for the day, or that you get your email under control for that day. Then, break it down hourly; by 9 am, you'll have your documentation ready for tomorrow's presentation, by 10 am, you'll have spoken to your boss about the presentation, by 11 am, you'll have called that important customer about their request for more information ... you get the picture.

Have goals for everything you do, both in your business and your personal life. Again, your goals don't have to be major, I'M GOING TO DO THIS AND THEN I'LL BE SUCCESSFUL-type goals. They need to be small, very achievable goals so you can feel in control of what's going on around you. Make them reasonable. Make them happen.

<u>Put your internal procrastinator in "time out."</u> We all have an internal procrastinator; you know, that guy in your head who says, "I can do this tomorrow." "It doesn't have to be done right now." "I  have time before the deadline; why rush?" Give him the pink slip – it's time to take back that control and reach your goals. You can do it!

Putting something off only adds anxiety and stress. We all procrastinate from time to time - it could be a chronic issue for some while for others; it's only a problem in certain areas of their life. Procrastination is frustrating because it creates a domino effect in wasted time, lost opportunities, disappointing work performance, and generally a bad perceived feeling of self.

Procrastinating allows less important things to take over your time and space. Most people don't have a problem finding time for the things they want to do, but once we think of a task as challenging, time consuming, or boring, we'd rather not do it and procrastination takes over.

"Procrastination is the thief of the future." Edward Young

4 THE PLANNING PROCESS

The goal with time management is to make the process seamless, stress-free and easy to maintain; otherwise, it'll go by the wayside. Remember, though, that it takes doing the same thing 21 times before it becomes a habit, and really, what we're establishing is a time habit, like eating healthy or having a budget; if you skip a day or change your pattern, you'll have to start all over again with setting new priorities.

Start by making an appointment with yourself each day to plan. Write it down on your calendar; it doesn't matter what type of calendar you use, just make sure you write it in there. I typically set aside 30 minutes each morning and 30 minutes at the end of each work day to go through each day's priorities and the priorities for the next day, as well as going through my email to make sure it's cleaned up, filed and ready to move forward. By actually making that appointment with yourself, you're proving to yourself that your time is valuable, like a doctor's appointment – if you miss it, it could lead to an unhealthy, stressful situation and you don't want to go back there.

<u>Use your calendar</u>. Again, it doesn't matter what type of calendar you use; I have 4 calendars I use so I always know what's going on when. I have an electronic calendar on my computer that syncs with my mobile devices. I also have a hard copy calendar (I use a DayTimer, but you can use whatever works best for you), where I write everything down each day as it goes along, a desk calendar for the day and a full-desk calendar that shows me the month at a glance. By keeping my priorities, appointments and deadlines in front of me at all times, in one form or another, I stay on task and am able to move through my goals consistently and in a timely fashion.

<u>Break down each task into smaller steps</u>. It's so easy to get bogged down and stressed out when you take a look at all the things you have to accomplish. It's like looking at an elephant and thinking, "I'll never be able to eat that whole thing." But remember – you eat an elephant one bite at a time. That major project that has to be done is just a series of small steps, so break it down into those steps and set each step as a goal. As you accomplish each of the smaller goals, you'll feel as if you're really getting things done and your stress level will go down. Before you know it, as you get more and more smaller goals taken care of, your whopper of a project is done!

<u>Schedule the routine things first</u>. When you're looking at your daily plan, make sure to put your routine obligations down first; if you have regularly-standing conference calls or meetings, make sure those are down on the plan first. If you have tasks that need to be done every day, write those down too.

Set your "Do" priority list:

- ✓ Must Do
- ✓ Should Do
- ✓ Can Do

Your "Must Do" list are the top 5 things you absolutely, without fail, have to accomplish that day. It would include your routine meetings, calls and tasks, as well as the urgent items that cannot wait another day.

Your "Should Do" list are those things that should be done today but if they don't get done, the world won't come crashing down around you. These 5 or 6 items would typically move up to "Must Do" status in the next few days.

The "Can Do" list are those things that need to get done but can wait until you've gotten everything else accomplished. They will eventually catch fire and move up the list, but for now, they're things that can typically wait.

Keep you "Do" lists simple, no more than 5 or 6 items in each category; remember that if everything is urgent, then nothing is urgent. Really look at your priorities and make critical judgments about where they belong on the "Do" list each day to avoid feeling overloaded.

5 PUTTING IT INTO PRACTICE

Step 1 – Getting Into Gear

Salesmen will say that the hardest door to open is your front door and the same is true when it comes to time management – as a manager, the hardest person to manage is yourself. So get going!

Make your appointment to plan and really use it to plan. Each morning, take that time to go through your "Do" list. Make it clear and concise. Work through it throughout the day and then at the end of your day, keep your second appointment to go through your day's list, recognize your accomplishments for the day and set priorities for the next day.

By recognizing what you've gotten done each day, you end the day on a positive note, you feel as though you've had a modicum of control over your day and you can go into your "life" time feeling less stressed.

By setting tomorrow's goals the night before, you start each day feeling as though you've got a handle on the coming day and you don't dread the day to come before you even enter the office. But remember – going over your next day's plan the night before doesn't mean you can skip the morning appointment. Overnight, emails continue to come in, priorities can change and the world moves forward, so your goals for the day may change when you first get it. Make sure to keep both the morning and evening appointments with yourself each day to stay on top of shifting priorities and continue to feel in control.

To sum it up:

- ✓ Set aside specific time for your routine things that need to be done daily/weekly. At that time, turn off your email and IM and just get it done.
- ✓ Set a goal of what you need to accomplish that week.
- ✓ Divide your weekly goal by your potential work hours for how much time the routine things will take and how much time is left over during the week.
- ✓ Decrease desktop clutter
- ✓ File or discard papers and folders
- ✓ Purge outdated materials, manuals, scraps of paper in your drawers
- ✓ Update customer management database with ALL client/prospect data and discard associated paper
- ✓ Assign a place for everything and keep everything in its place
- ✓ File as you go, don't wait until "sometime" to put things in their place
- ✓ Organize your workspace for maximum productivity
- ✓ Reserve your inbox for action items
- ✓ Create email folders to organize your inbox and sent emails

✓ Break down large projects into smaller tasks, and prioritize them. Block off time each day until the project is completed

✓ All projects and tasks should have clear goals, objectives, and deadlines

✓ Plan your "Do" list for the following day before you leave work

✓ Enter calls and appointments into your calendar

✓ Schedule a break to refresh and refocus, without interruptions.

✓ Schedule at least 1 hour per day for NO technology: don't answer phones, respond to emails or engage in office communication. Take this time to regroup and work on pressing issues, modify your "Do" list and work on projects.

Step 2 – Teamwork

None of us work in a vacuum; we have others around us and whether we're worker bees or managers, we need to work well with others to accomplish the bigger goals.

The biggest challenge most of us face is that we're critical of our co-workers; this guy isn't pulling his weight, that woman is annoying, no one does their job as well as I do and I'm always picking up the slack – you know the drill.

Well, stop it. Remember that no one comes into the office each day intending to slack off, any more than you do. Your problem with your co-workers is your problem but it can become a company-wide problem if it's stopping you from getting the job done.

It's important to work as a team with those around you. You're all working toward the same goal, so stop looking at others as if they're out to get you; they may be, but the best way to avoid them succeeding is by working with them toward the common goal of getting the job done.

The guy not pulling his weight? He may have a time management problem, the same as you do; he's overwhelmed by having too much to do and not enough control over it. The annoying woman in the next cubicle? Perhaps she doesn't know how to set priorities well, so she's constantly asking questions.

The best leaders are those who help others be better – whether you're a manager or not, you still accomplish more by working well with your co-workers, helping them accomplish more. This isn't a competition – it's a cooperation and a corporation.

Making the most of your time and effort is key to success. There are only so many hours in the day to work and by only using YOUR time, you can only accomplish so much. When you choose to include others' time through delegation, you magnify your productivity and efficiency.

Quick tips:

1. Eliminate unnecessary activities
2. Prioritize so you focus your energy on tasks that provide the highest rate of return
3. Set long and short-term goals with action steps for the team, motivating everyone to keep on target
4. Effectively delegate. Are you the only person to do this task or can someone else do it more efficiently while you take care of more important things?
5. Outsource non-core tasks/projects either within the organization or to an outside contractor (if allowed).

Step 3 – Email

Oh my. Email and computers were supposed to make things easier but they've ended up generating more paper and wasting more of our time than every could have been imagined. And chances are, if your office email is out of control, you also have a pile of regular mail sitting on your dining room table or kitchen counter at home, so the principles apply equally to email and snail mail.

In 2011, it was estimated that there were 3.146 billion email accounts and 2.8 million emails sent and received every day. Wow!

Have you ever spent wasted minutes or hours feverishly searching for an email that contains an important document? It becomes a frustrating unproductive endeavor that is a misuse of your valuable time AND time is money.

Staying on top of your email is critical to keeping your time under control. Without good email management, you'll constantly be looking for things, jumping to attention with each email and being continually distracted by what's coming next, instead of focusing on the tasks at hand.

So how do you get your email under control? Focus. Manage your email the same as you manage your time, with planning.

Not every email is urgent. The world will not end if you don't answer an email within 5 minutes of receiving it, so let your email flow throughout the day and check it as you complete each task.

<u>Manage your email inbox; set aside time to answer emails other than your daily work time</u>. Again, using your 30 minutes of planning time in the morning and evening will help keep your email under control. Use 15 minutes of that time to go through your emails, file them, add important ones to your "Do" list or otherwise delete it.

The best way of managing your inbox is to use the 1-touch rule: touch each email only once, deal with it and then file/delete it. But remember to do this only during your planning time; throughout the day, let the email just flow through and pick up the ones that are truly urgent, in line with your "Do" list.

Set up folders according to importance:
- ✓ Emails from your boss;
- ✓ Project-specific emails;
- ✓ Company-specific emails;
- ✓ Client-specific emails.

Each email can then be sent to the specific folder to be dealt with at its appropriate time; it stops the constant "ping-ping-ping-ping" of emails coming in, like someone dropping beads of water onto your forehead.

As you set up your folders, also set up email rules that allow each one to go directly into the folders instead of going into your inbox; rules keep things organized and allow you to deal with things as they come up on your "Do" list, instead of as they come into your inbox.

The one caveat with rules is to make sure not to automatically file emails that might be urgent, like emails from the company president. You can add, change or delete email rules as projects and priorities require, so remember that, just because something is set up as a rule, it's not set in concrete.

Some additional important points:

- ✓ Schedule 2-3 times during the day to check/respond to emails
- ✓ Turn off notifications at other times
- ✓ If you have emails delivered on your Smartphone, either turn off the sounds or designate particular tones for personal or business related emails.
- ✓ Create an autoresponder stating that you check your emails X amount of times per day and you will respond within 24 hours. If it is urgent, please call _____.

Step 4 – Cleanup

Before you can truly be organized, you do have to go through a clean up the mess you've gotten yourself into. Remember – it's an elephant, but it can be eaten, one bite at a time.

<u>Delete clutter</u>, both in your cyber world and your real world. If your office is cluttered and full of miscellaneous paper, you're going to feel more stress and less able to focus. The more "stuff" you collect, the more cluttered your mind becomes. It goes beyond the Feng Shui of life and relates to emotional and physical space. It can seem a daunting task if you have created an overload of things, but as you begin to discard and organize, you create more mind space as well.

<u>Use the same 1-touch policy for paper as you do for email;</u> touch each piece of paper or mail once, deal with it and be done with it.

- ✓ Create folders and sub-folders
- ✓ Use short names
- ✓ Be diligent about filing
- ✓ Separate current and completed works
- ✓ Archive older, unneeded documents – store in a separate folder, USB or cloud storage
- ✓ Create shortcuts or links to documents you use more consistently. Maintaining a single copy ensures you are always using the most current version.
- ✓ Delete unnecessary files

✓ Create shortcuts of your most used documents and save them on your desktop.

✓ If you routinely share documents with a group, consider using Google Docs, Teambox, Dropbox or another online sharing tool for collaborating.

Don't wait for someone else to make suggestions on how to manage your time better; take the initiative and share with others ideas that work for you.

Taking the time to organize and streamline your office operations, even if it is just your email and documents, help to increase your efficiency and productivity – which saves you time and money. The less time you must spend scavenging through folders and emails, the more time you have to devote to important business tasks and daily procedures.

6 TIME MANAGEMENT – FINAL THOUGHTS

Final thoughts to help you get things back under control:

✓ Make sure to schedule time for yourself and stick to it.
✓ Manage both your work and life obligations the same.
✓ Keep a time log for a week or 2 to see where your time is going – you'll be surprised.
✓ Managing your time will help prevent burnout and stress because you're in control.

The mightiest wave begins with a single drop.

Organization and time management skills are learned-following these steps will allow you to become more successful, streamlined, and proficient, and will reduce your stress, both at work and at home.

7 APPENDIX: TOOLS AND FORMS

We couldn't have you go away without giving you some forms that have worked well for us. Hope these help you get your time under your own control and get back on track to productivity!

Prioritizing your activities

	High Value (Very important)	**Low Value** (Not as important)
Deadline (High urgency)	1. Do it now! "Click here to add activities."	3. Gotta minute? "Click here to add activities."
No Deadline (Low urgency)	2. I really should... "Click here to add activities."	4. I really shouldn't... "Click here to add activities."

Time Management Log

Name _____   Month _____
Day _____   Year _____

Task List	8:00	9:00	10:00	11:00	12:00	1:00	2:00	3:00	4:00	5:00

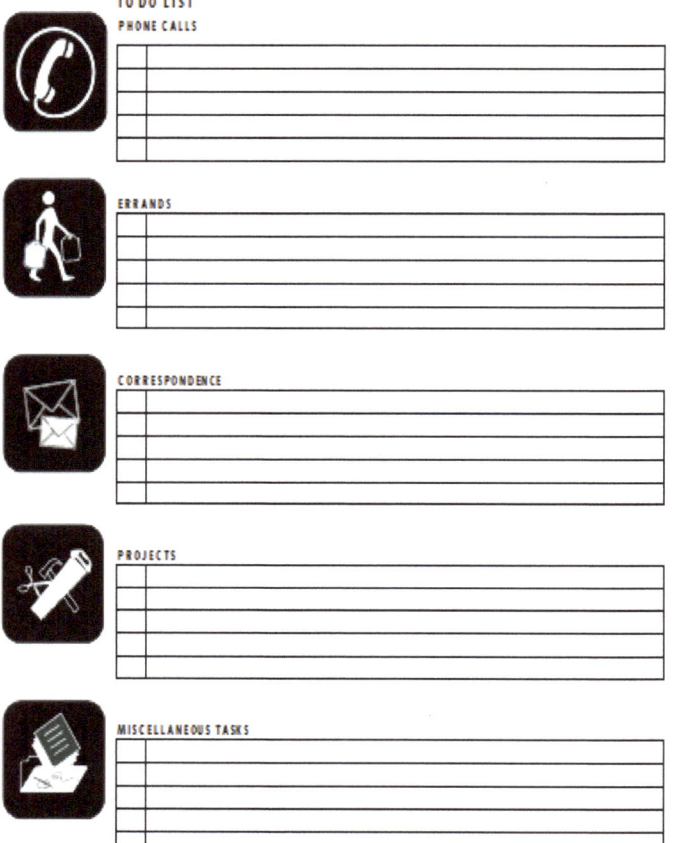

TO DO LIST

PHONE CALLS

ERRANDS

CORRESPONDENCE

PROJECTS

MISCELLANEOUS TASKS

ABOUT THE AUTHORS

Laurie Leiker has spent 20 years as a corporate consultant, helping grow new managers into strong, effective leaders. Author of "Help! My Email Is Ruling My Life!" and "Motivating Feedback: Getting The Most From Your Employees," Laurie lives in Austin, Texas and is a grateful breast cancer survivor.

Susan Poirier, Owner/Consultant of Ace Concierge LLC: With 30 years of experience in business, Suzie has been the executive assistant for hundreds of businesses and entrepreneurs nationwide. Her enthusiasm, energy, wit and dedication to time management and productivity, deliver the kind of exemplary service business owners need and depend upon in a person who keeps them organized, efficient and free to focus on their core genius. She has been working independently for over 12 years with entrepreneurs from Canada to Florida, providing a wide range of virtual administrative skills from executive admin tasks and social media management to travel planning, and presentations. The service solutions are only limited by her client's requests. Working virtually, her extensive experience, support and knowledge has helped numerous entrepreneurs achieve their success and business goals.

www.ingramcontent.com/pod-product-compliance
Lightning Source LLC
Chambersburg PA
CBHW041117180526
45172CB00001B/302